REDEFINED
A Journey of Identity, Healing, and
Freedom in Christ

Paulette Toews

"If you want to see God do something impossible in your life, you have to open your heart and mind to God's vision for your life."

Author Unknown

"I waited patiently for the Lord; he turned to me and heard my cry. He lifted me out of the slimy pit, out of the mud and mire; he set my feet on a rock and gave me a firm place to stand. He put a new song in my mouth, a hymn of praise to our God. Many will see and fear and put their trust in the Lord."
Psalm 40:1–3

Dedications

Yvonne Van Dellen
When I was deeply broken and could not see a way forward, your faithfulness and love for Christ held space for my life. You stayed, you loved, and you believed when I could not.

Because of you, I lived long enough for Jesus to grab my heart.

Lana Sewell
My sister-in-law and sister friend. Thank you for being a steady presence throughout this journey—for praying with me and for me, for listening through long hours of struggle and frustration, and for walking faithfully beside me in every season.

"Thank you" doesn't even begin to cover it.
I love you both.

Introduction

How I Learned My Feelings Were Lying

For a long time, I found myself living with two different beliefs. I knew in my head that God's Word was true, but in my heart, I listened to the voice of shame. I loved Jesus and did my best to serve Him, trusting Him with my eternity, but when it came to my identity, I struggled. I knew God loved me, He loves everyone, but I wasn't sure if He liked me, or if He wanted anything to do with me. Deep down, I carried questions I was afraid to say out loud. Why do I still feel broken if God has forgiven me? Why am I still scared if I belong to Him? Why do I feel unworthy if He calls me loved? I knew all the right answers, but my feelings kept telling me a different story. And for a long time, I let those feelings have the final word.

This book was born in that space between what I knew in my head and what I doubted in my heart. It started with the quiet realization that you can know God's Word is true and still live under the heavy weight of a mistaken identity. I had learned how to survive. I had learned how to keep going. I had learned how to serve others. But I hadn't yet learned how to rest in who I was in Christ. What I eventually discovered, and what I hold onto now is this: How I feel does not reflect the truth. Not because feelings don't matter, but because they were never meant to be the boss of my identity.

Identity is more important than we sometimes realize. If the enemy can twist how, you see yourself, he can quietly affect how you love, trust, receive, forgive, obey, and even how you belong. When identity is shaky, everything else feels fragile. You might love God but find yourself living guarded. You might believe Scripture but still feel disqualified. You might know you're forgiven but still feel condemned. You might be adopted but live like an orphan. You might be free but still feel trapped. I wrote this because so many of us live in that tension, we love Jesus, but we still carry lies about ourselves.

This isn't a self-help book, a quick-fix guide, or a psychology manual. It's a Christ-centered journey to help restore your identity. Together, we'll look at God's original design for you, how identity can be broken by sin and pain, what it means to be made new in Christ, why forgiveness is so important for freedom, how adoption heals the orphan heart, and how to walk in daily freedom. This book won't rush you, won't shame you, and won't ignore your pain. Instead, it will invite you into truth, healing, freedom, and real transformation.

If your identity has been shaped by abuse, abandonment, rejection, betrayal, neglect, or hidden shame, I want you to know this book is for you. What happened to you matters. It really does. But it does not get to define you. Only Jesus does.

You don't have to read this all at once. You don't have to "do it right." You don't even have to feel ready. All you need is a willing heart and an honest spirit. Some chapters might feel comforting. Others might feel a little uncomfortable. Some may bring hope. Others may feel tender. Let the Holy Spirit set the pace for you. Pause when you need to. Pray when you feel stirred. Come back when you're ready. This isn't a race. It's a return.

I didn't write this as someone who has it all together. I've wrestled with shame, walked through brokenness, learned forgiveness the hard way, discovered adoption after abandonment, and I'm still learning how to walk in freedom. This isn't just my story. It's about what Jesus does with stories like ours.

As you begin Chapter One, I invite you to be open. You don't have to have everything figured out. You don't have to be fully healed or fearless. You just need to be willing.

Before we go any further, please hear this: you are not an accident. You are not forgotten. You are not disqualified. You are not too broken. You are deeply known, fully loved, and already being restored.

Let's begin.

Created in the Image:

Designed, Not Defined

Before anything went wrong, before shame had a chance to speak, before fear told you to hide, before trauma touched your story, God had already spoken your identity over you. That matters more than you realize.

We live in a world that is obsessed with identity. Everyone is searching for it, trying to define it, reshape it, and defend it. We're told to "find ourselves," "be our truth," and decide who we are, then expect everyone else to agree. But Scripture doesn't tell us to invent our identity. It says identity is received, not created. You don't find out who you are by looking inward, but by listening to the One who made you.

"So God created man in His own image, in the image of God He created them." (Genesis 1:27)

That single verse confronts so many of the lies we have lived under. You are not self-made. You are not accidental. You are not the result of chance. You are not an afterthought. You exist because God chose to speak you into being.

When God says, "Let Us make man in Our image," He means it with purpose. Before the oceans existed, before the stars were counted, before history began, God had you in mind. Scripture also says:

"God saw all that He had made, and it was very good." (Genesis 1:31)

Before you struggled, failed, or anything happened to you, God already called you very good.

This means shame is not your original state. Brokenness is not your identity. Fear is not where you belong. Trauma is not your real story. Redemption doesn't create your worth; it restores what was always there.

If Satan wanted to destroy humanity, he didn't have to start with behavior. He only had to start with identity. Once identity is confused, behavior follows. That's why the enemy's first attack in the garden was not about obedience, but about trust in who God said they were. That same struggle continues today. The enemy doesn't need to convince you that God isn't real. He just needs to make you believe God loves others more, your past disqualifies you, your wounds define you, your struggle means something is wrong with you, or your shame is your name. Slowly, people stop living from what God says and start living from what they feel. That's where mistaken identity begins.

Some of us learned to treat feelings as truth. But Scripture teaches something stronger. Feelings describe what we experience; truth declares who we are. You can feel unwanted and still be chosen, feel forgotten and still be remembered, feel broken and still be whole, feel like too much and still be deeply desired, or feel like not enough and still be fully sufficient in Christ. One of the enemy's most dangerous lies isn't "God isn't real," but "This is just who you are now." Little by little, people start living from pain instead of promise, from memory instead of truth, from what happened instead of what God has said.

That's why this confession is so important on this journey: How I feel does not reflect the truth. I'm not saying feelings don't matter, but they are not the final authority over who I am.

Some people struggle with identity because of confusion, others because of harm. Some wounds come from being sinned against, abuse, violation, abandonment, betrayal, neglect. These wounds do more than hurt emotionally, they try to rewrite identity. Trauma whispers lies like, "My body is not safe," "My voice doesn't matter," "I must be the problem," "God must not have been there." But let this be said clearly and gently: what happened to you is not who you are. It violated your identity; it did not create it. Your worth was not altered by what was done to you. Your purity was not erased by what was taken from you. Your future was not canceled by what tried to destroy you. Jesus does not minimize what happened, but He also refuses to let it become your name.

This chapter isn't asking who you have been, what has happened to you, or what you struggle with. It's asking something much deeper: Who did God say you were before any of that ever touched your life? Because healing doesn't begin with your wound. It starts with your design.

Take a moment. Don't rush. Ask yourself honestly: When did you stop believing you were "very good"? Whose voice became louder than God's? What label do you fear losing the most? What identity do you hide behind to feel safe? You don't need to fix anything yet. You only need to notice.

Before moving forward, I encourage you to pray.
Father, before I bring You my wounds, my questions, or my shame, I receive what You spoke first. I was created by You. I was seen by You. I was called "very good" by You. I choose to begin this journey not with what broke me, but with what You designed. Teach my heart how to listen again. In Jesus' name, Amen.

Here's the truth I want you to carry with you into the next chapter: **You are not**

starting from brokenness. You are
returning to design.

CHAPTER TWO

The Fracture:

When Shame Became a Voice

No one is born hiding. We are born reaching, crying, trusting, and looking for connection. Hiding is learned. Somewhere along the way, something happens, and the instinct to be known is replaced by the instinct to self-protect. A moment, a season, a wound, a betrayal, a violation, a disappointment, a failure, and suddenly openness feels dangerous. Vulnerability feels costly. Trust feels risky. This is where the fracture begins. Not when sin first appears in your own life, but when shame first learns your name.

Genesis 3 is not just ancient history. It is the mirror of every human soul. Before this moment, there was no shame, no fear, no self-consciousness, no need to cover up, and no instinct to hide. Scripture says,

"Then the eyes of both of them were opened, and they realized they were naked; so they sewed fig

leaves together and made coverings for themselves" (Genesis 3:7)

The first response to sin was not repentance. It was covering. Then God comes into the garden and asks a question that has echoed through every generation since:

"Where are you?" (Genesis 3:9)

God was not confused about Adam and Eve's location. He was exposing the shift that had taken place inside them. They were no longer standing where they once stood, in trust, openness, and belonging. They were now standing in fear. And Adam answers with words that still describe the human condition: *"I was afraid… so I hid."* Sin gave birth to fear. Fear gave birth to shame. Shame gave birth to hiding. And hiding gave birth to mistaken identity.

Shame doesn't say, "You made a mistake." Shame says, "You are the mistake." And that's what makes it so dangerous, because it doesn't just address what you did, it attacks who you are. But that's not how God speaks. When the Holy Spirit brings conviction, He doesn't shame you. Conviction points to what you did. Shame attacks who you are. Conviction says, "Come back." Shame says, "Stay away." Conviction invites you into the light. Shame runs from it. That's why shame never just affects what you do, it reshapes how you see yourself. You don't just feel bad about what happened. You start to believe something is wrong with you. Sometimes those beliefs come from your own choices. Other times, they come from what was done to us. Abuse. Violation. Abandonment. Neglect. Betrayal. Silence. Being left. Being used. Being unseen. These wounds don't just hurt the heart; they try to rewrite identity. Trauma whispers lies like: "My body is not safe," "My voice does not matter," "I must have caused this," "God must not have been there," and "This is just who I am now."

For many years, I didn't realize that what had happened to me had quietly changed how I saw myself. I knew my story. I knew the events. I even knew the Scriptures. But I didn't yet understand how deeply shame had attached itself to my identity. I learned how to survive before I ever learned how to feel safe. I learned how to function before I learned how to rest. I learned how to smile before I learned how to be honest. There were seasons when I loved Jesus sincerely, but still lived from fear, performance, and self-protection. I didn't call it shame back then. I called it "being strong." I called it "being independent." I called it "just pushing through." But underneath all of that, there was a quiet, persistent question I didn't know how to name: What is wrong with me? That's the question shame always leaves behind.

Once shame takes hold, hiding feels necessary. You hide your questions, your fears, your anger, your confusion, your pain, and your struggle. Not because you don't want help, but because you're afraid of what will happen if you're fully known. For a long time, hiding felt like wisdom to me. It felt like protection. It felt like control. But hiding always costs you intimacy. And over time, you forget that hiding was a response to pain. It just becomes your way of life. You don't say, "I hide." You just live guarded.

The Bible never calls the wounded "ruined." It calls them brokenhearted, crushed in spirit, captive, bound, afflicted. And to every one of those conditions, God attaches a promise of healing, restoration, freedom, and redemption.

"The Lord is close to the brokenhearted." (Psalm 34:18)

"He heals the brokenhearted and binds up their wounds." (Psalm 147:3)

This became one of the most important discoveries of my healing: God does not recoil from fracture. He draws near to it.

There were years when my feelings had more authority in my life than Scripture. I felt ashamed, unworthy, discarded, and too broken to fix. And because those feelings were so strong, I believed they must be true. But healing began when this one truth finally settled in my heart: How I feel does not reflect the truth. Not because feelings don't matter, but because they are not allowed to be the boss of my identity. Feelings describe what I experience. Truth declares who I am. I could feel ashamed and still be clean. I could feel abandoned and still be chosen. I could feel broken and still be redeemable. That truth didn't silence every feeling overnight, but it broke their authority.

Take a breath. Let this be gentle. Ask yourself: Where did shame first attach itself to your identity? What lie have you repeated so long that it feels like truth? Where do you still feel the instinct to hide? What do you fear being fully known for? You're not trying to fix anything yet. You're just noticing what's there.

Before we move forward, let's pray.

Jesus, You see the places where shame entered. You see the moments that changed how I saw myself. You see what I hid because it felt safer than being known. I bring You the fear. I bring You the confusion. I bring You the fracture. I renounce the lie that what happened to me defines who I am. I release the belief that I am too broken to be restored. Speak truth where shame once lived. Bring light where fear once ruled. I choose truth. In Your name, Amen.

Here's the truth I want you to carry with you into the next chapter: **You are not defined by the fracture. You are defined by the One who stepped into it to redeem you.**

CHAPTER THREE

New Creation:

When My Old Name Lost Its Power

Shame tells you who you were. Fear tells you who you might become. Trauma tells you who you are not. But the gospel tells you something far more radical: you are not who you were. Christianity is not about self-improvement. It is about death and resurrection. We do not become better versions of our old selves; we become new creations.

"Therefore, if anyone is in Christ, he is a new creation; the old has gone, the new has come!" *(2 Corinthians 5:17)*

That verse sounds simple, but it carries the weight of a funeral and a resurrection at the same time. Something really does die in Christ. And something entirely new really does live.

One of the most powerful phrases in the New Testament is only two words long: *in*

Christ. It means your life is no longer centered on your past, your wounds, your failures, your trauma, or your regrets. Your life is now centered in His life, His righteousness, His victory, and His resurrection.

"I have been crucified with Christ and I no longer live, but Christ lives in me" (Galatians 2:20)

That does not mean your personality disappears. It does not mean your memories vanish. It does not mean your story is erased. It means your source has changed. Shame is no longer your source. Fear is no longer your source. Trauma is no longer your source. Christ is.

There was a season when I knew I loved Jesus, but I still lived as if my past had more authority than His cross. I believed I was forgiven. I believed He was my Savior. But I hadn't yet learned how to live as though my old identity was actually dead. I didn't say it out loud, but my life kept repeating old messages, be careful, don't trust too much, stay guarded, don't hope too boldly. I could talk about new life and still live from self-protection. I could quote Scripture and still let fear make my decisions. What I didn't realize at the time was this: I believed I was forgiven, but I wasn't yet living as though I had been reborn.

Paul doesn't say our old self is weak. He says it was crucified. *"We know that our old self was crucified with Him"* (Romans 6:6). Crucified means executed, finished, no longer in charge. But here's the tension every believer faces, dead things still try to talk. Old habits whisper. Old fears call your name. Old patterns feel familiar. Old reactions try to rise. But just because something feels familiar doesn't mean it has authority. Just because something sounds like you does not mean it still gets to define you.

When I was about eight years old, I began being called by a different name. I didn't choose it, but I embraced it. I didn't understand it. It simply started happening in my world. A man who worked with my dad, and later became part of our home, began calling me Pete instead of Paulette.

At that age, I didn't have words for what it meant or why it mattered. I only know this now: something in me quietly separated. My given name, the one I had always been called, slowly faded into the background. And a new name, one I never asked for but again, embraced, took its place.

Looking back with the eyes of healing, I can see something I could not see then. I didn't just carry a different name. I had a different sense of self. That name became attached to survival, to confusion, to fear I didn't yet know how to name, to a world that no longer felt simple or safe. Years later, when I became a follower of Jesus, something holy and unmistakable began to happen. As He started restoring what had been broken, I quietly returned to my real name, Paulette. No announcement. No ceremony. Just a steady reclaiming of who I was beneath everything that had happened to me. And only much later did I understand the weight of that moment. Pete belonged to a season of survival. Paulette belongs to resurrection. I didn't choose the first renaming, but I did receive the second one. And in that reclaiming, Jesus was not just saving me; He was giving me back to myself.

For a long time, my prayers were mostly about getting through the day, the emotions, the memories, and the heaviness. And God was faithful in that season. He carried me. But there came a moment when the Holy Spirit began to shift my prayers gently. I was no longer just asking for survival. I was being invited into identity. Not "help me endure," but "teach me who I am now." And that was a new kind of healing. Not just learning that I was safe but learning that I was new.

Some people worry that if they fully embrace being a new creation, they'll be denying their story. But a new creation doesn't erase your memories; it just removes their power to define you. You may still remember what happened, but now memory is a witness, not a master. Trauma may still explain why your body reacts, but it doesn't get to define who you are. Your nervous system may still remember, but your spirit has already been made new. Healing is often the process of your soul learning what your spirit already knows. There were days when I still felt like my old self. Days when fear felt louder than faith. Days when shame still tried to rise. I learned something important in that season: feelings are powerful communicators, but terrible authorities. That's when this confession became more than just a phrase to me. It became a lifeline: **How I feel does not reflect the truth.** I could feel afraid and still be secure. I could feel unsure and still be chosen. I could feel weak and still be alive in Christ. That truth didn't silence every emotion overnight, but it taught me which voice was allowed to lead.

Take a quiet moment and ask yourself: Where do you still introduce yourself by who you used to be? What old label still feels more familiar than "new creation"? Where do you still live as though the cross didn't finish the work? You're not condemning yourself. You're just noticing where resurrection is still unfolding. Before we move forward, let's pray.

Jesus, I believe You did not only forgive my sins, you replaced my life. I believe my old self was crucified with You. I believe Your resurrection life now lives in me. Where my past still speaks louder than Your cross, silence it. Where my fear still tries to lead, remove its authority. Where my shame still tries to name me, rename me. I receive my new life. I receive my new identity. I receive Your resurrection power in me. In Your loving name, Amen.

Here's the truth I want you to carry with you into the next chapter: **Forgiveness releases the past, but new creation redefines the future.**

CHAPTER FOUR

Forgiven and Forgiving:

When I Laid Down My Right to Hold On

There is a moment in every healing journey when the question is no longer, *did this hurt?* The question becomes, *what will I do with what hurt me?* Forgiveness is often the place where people either step fully into freedom or stay standing at the doorway, uncertain and afraid. Not because they don't love God. Not because they don't want to be healed. But because forgiveness feels like the most misunderstood, misused, and emotionally loaded word in the Christian life.

For some, forgiveness was demanded too early. For others, it was weaponized. For many, it was confused with silence, endurance, or pretending it didn't matter. But biblical forgiveness is none of those things. Forgiveness is not saying what happened didn't matter. It is not calling evil "okay." It is not trusting someone who is not safe. It is not removing boundaries. It is not automatically restoring the relationship. It is not forgetting. It is not minimizing your pain. And it is not pretending justice doesn't matter. Forgiveness does not deny the wrong. It faces the wrong and then chooses not to let it remain your master.

At its core, forgiveness is this: releasing someone from your courtroom and placing them into God's hands. It is not excusing. It is releasing. Jesus said,

"Forgive, and you will be forgiven" (Luke 6:37),

and Paul wrote,

"Forgive as the Lord forgave you."
(Colossians 3:13)

Forgiveness is not rooted in what the offender deserves. It is rooted in what Christ has already done.

Forgiveness feels dangerous because it feels like letting go of control, the right to be angry, the right to demand repayment, and the right to hold someone accountable with your own hands. And for those who have been wounded deeply, forgiveness can feel like asking the impossible. It can sound like: "If I let this go, then what protected me all these years?" But here's the truth, most people only discover after they forgive: bitterness doesn't protect you. It imprisons you. It feels like strength, but it quietly steals your peace, your clarity, your joy, and your sense of safety.

For a long time, I believed in forgiveness, but I didn't yet live in it. I knew Jesus had forgiven me. I taught about grace. I could even pray for others. But when it came to the people and circumstances that had wounded me most deeply, forgiveness felt terrifying. Not because I didn't understand Scripture, but because I was afraid of what I would lose if I let go. I didn't realize yet that what I would lose was only the chain.

I wrestled. I delayed. I justified my anger. I told myself I wasn't ready. And in one sense, that was true. Forgiveness isn't meant to be rushed. God is patient with our process. He is gentle with our fear. But there came a moment when the Holy Spirit made something very clear to me: You're *not protecting yourself anymore. You're protecting the wound.* When that became clear, I didn't feel relief, I felt fear. Holding on had become familiar. Anger had become a strange kind of companion. "Letting go felt like stepping off a ledge without knowing what was beneath me. I wanted to believe God would be there, but in that moment, I wasn't sure. And I was terrified of who I would be without the armor I had built out of pain."

One of the greatest misunderstandings about forgiveness is this: people think they must feel forgiving before they can forgive. But Scripture reveals the opposite order. Forgiveness begins with a decision of obedience, not an emotion of relief. Jesus forgave while nails were still in His hands, while betrayal was still fresh, and while mockery was still in the air. Forgiveness did not wait for healing. Forgiveness created the way for it.

There came a time when I knew I could no longer carry what I was holding. I didn't need another teaching. I needed a moment of release that matched the weight of what I had been carrying. So, I did something very simple and not really holy. I wrote a letter. Not to send. Not to explain. Not to reopen communication. But to name the truth. I wrote what happened. I wrote what it cost me. I wrote what I felt. I wrote what I lost. And then I wrote what I was choosing: *I release you. You no longer get to define me.* And when I was ready, I placed that letter into a fire and watched it burn. It wasn't dramatic. It wasn't emotional at first. But it was final. And something in me knew, *this no longer owns me.*

If you're willing, when the time is right, I invite you to consider the same act. Not as a ritual. Not as a requirement. But as a response. Write what you need to say. Speak what was never safe to speak. Name what was real. And then, when you're ready, release it. Let the fire burn away what you no longer need to hold. This isn't for the offender. This is for your freedom.

This must be said clearly and kindly: you can forgive and still maintain boundaries. You can forgive and still choose to keep your distance. You can forgive and still call out what was wrong. You can forgive and still protect your heart. Forgiveness heals your soul. Reconciliation requires two healed hearts.

Forgiveness didn't erase my memories. But it did erase their authority. The anger lost its grip. The rehearsals slowed. The tightness in my chest eased. The flash of fear softened. And for the first time, I could say honestly, *what happened to me is part of my story, but it is no longer my prison.*

If you're willing, ask yourself: Who are you still carrying in your heart? What offense still feels "unfair" to release? Where do you still feel justified in holding on? What might freedom look like if you let go? There's no condemnation here. Only invitation. Let's pray.

Jesus, I bring You the weight I have carried. I bring You the anger I learned to live with. I bring You the names I still hold tightly in my heart. I do not excuse what was done, but I choose to release what no longer belongs in my hands. I place justice back into Your care. I place my wounds into Your healing. I choose freedom. In Your freeing name, Amen.

Here's the truth I want you to carry with you into the next chapter: **Forgiveness breaks the chain, but belonging is what fills the space it leaves behind.**

CHAPTER FIVE

Cherished & Adopted:

When I Stopped Living Like an Orphan

Forgiveness breaks chains, but it does not automatically teach the heart how to belong. Many people are freed from the prison of their past only to quietly continue living as though they are still alone in the world. They are forgiven but not yet resting. Healed, but not yet at home. Free, but not yet convinced they are wanted. This is where adoption becomes more than theology. This is where it becomes identity.

There's a difference between being rescued and being chosen. Rescue saves you from danger. Adoption gives you a place at the table. Some of us know what it is to be rescued by Jesus, but we still live as though we could be sent away at any moment. We live grateful but guarded. Loved, but braced. Included, but never fully at ease. That's the language of an orphan heart.

An orphan heart says, *I must earn my place. I can't depend on anyone. If I'm too much, I'll be left. If I fail, I'll be replaced. If I'm fully known, I'll be rejected.* And that kind of heart can exist even inside the church. It can worship faithfully and still live braced for abandonment. But the gospel does not say we were merely tolerated. It says we were adopted.

"His unchanging plan has always been to adopt us into His own family by bringing us to Himself through Jesus Christ. And this gave Him great pleasure" (Ephesians 1:5 NLT)

Let that settle for a moment. God did not reluctantly take you in. He did not sigh and make room for you. He did not add you as an obligation. Your adoption gave Him great pleasure. Not obligation. Not duty. Not necessity. Delight.

Some people wrestle with feeling unwanted without knowing why. Others know exactly where that wound began, a parent who left, a home that fractured, a childhood marked by instability, a voice that should have stayed but didn't. Abandonment teaches a quiet, devastating lesson: *people leave.* And if that lesson goes unhealed, it often gets projected onto God. We trust Him as Savior but struggle to trust Him as Father. We believe He can redeem us, but we quietly wonder if He will stay.

God didn't just change your legal status. He changed your inner language.
"You did not receive a spirit that makes you a slave again to fear, but you received the Spirit of adoption by whom we cry out, 'Abba, Father'" (Romans 8:15 NLT)

Abba isn't a formal title. It's intimate. Tender. Relational. The Holy Spirit does more than tell you that you belong; He teaches your heart how to feel it. He begins to heal fear-based obedience, performance-driven faith, distance disguised as maturity, and independence mistaken for strength. And He teaches something far more vulnerable: dependence is safe here.

There was a season when I could say with confidence, "I know God forgives me," but I wasn't yet convinced He actually wanted me. I trusted His mercy more than I trusted His affection. I believed He kept me because of the cross, but I didn't yet know that He delighted in me because I was His. Slowly, gently, over time, the Spirit began to show me that God's love for me wasn't just legal. It was personal. Not just covenant, but compassion. Not just redemption, but relationship. And somewhere along the way, the orphan posture in my heart began to loosen its grip.

There was also a time when I did not struggle to believe God loved me, but I quietly struggled to believe He would stay. I trusted Him with my eternity more easily than I trusted Him with my attachment. Somewhere deep inside, I still lived with the expectation that love eventually leaves. What surprised me most in my healing was not a dramatic moment of belonging, but the slow, steady realization that God was not going anywhere. He was not waiting for me to fail. He was not growing tired of my process. He was not keeping a mental count of my weakness. He was simply present. And little by little, my heart learned a new language. Not survival. Not bracing. Not striving. Rest.

To be cherished means you are valued for who you are, not just what you produce. It means you are protected, not merely tolerated. It means you are desired, not simply included. It means you are enjoyed, not just endured. This is God's posture toward His children.

"See what great love the Father has lavished on us, that we should be called children of God! And that is what we are" (1 John 3:1 NLT)

Not what we might become. Not what we will be someday. What we are now!

Even after healing, even after forgiveness, even after new creation, the orphan voice can still try to whisper: *Don't need anyone. Stay guarded. Don't get your hopes up. Don't trust too deeply.* But the Spirit gently counters with a different voice: *You are safe. You are seen. You are secure. You are mine.* Belonging isn't learned in a moment. It's received over time.

Ask yourself honestly: Do you relate to God more as Master than as Father? Do you struggle to receive affection without suspicion? Do you feel safer producing than resting? Do you secretly believe you are easy to replace? There's no condemnation here. Only an invitation into deeper sonship and daughterhood. Let's pray.

Father, I receive what You have already given. I lay down the orphan heart. I release the fear of being left. I surrender the need to prove my worth. Teach my heart how to belong. Teach my soul how to rest. Teach my spirit how to receive love without flinching. I am not a guest. I am not an outsider. I am not on probation. I am Your child. In Jesus' name, Amen.

Here's the truth I want you to carry with you into the final chapter: **Forgiveness breaks chains. Adoption builds a home.**

CHAPTER SIX

Walking Free:

When Healing Became a Way of Life

Freedom is not a moment. It is a way of walking. There are powerful encounters with God that mark us forever, moments when chains fall, clarity comes, and release is real. But what determines the strength of those moments is not how intense they feel. It is how faithfully freedom is practiced afterward. Healing does not end when forgiveness begins. Identity does not finish forming the day we feel adopted. Freedom is not proven in one prayer. Freedom is learned through daily obedience.

Israel was delivered from Egypt in a night but learning how to live as free people took years. God can break chains instantly, but He teaches the soul how to walk free over time.

"It is for freedom that Christ has set us free" *(Galatians 5:1)*

That means we don't fight for freedom; we fight from freedom. Old patterns may still try to rise. Old fears may still speak. Old reactions may still surface. But they don't get to lead anymore.

You no longer live from who hurt you, who left you, what happened to you, or what you survived. You now live from who redeemed you, who named you, who adopted you, and who dwells in you. The gospel is not just about where you will go someday. It is about who you are becoming now.

Freedom is precious, and what is precious must be guarded. This doesn't mean fear-based protection. It means wise stewardship. You begin to learn which voices build your faith, which environments weaken your peace, which relationships draw you toward Christ, and which patterns pull you backward. Boundaries aren't walls; they're gates that protect what God has rebuilt.

There was a time when my reclaimed identity felt tender and honest, but still vulnerable. I was learning how to live as the person Jesus had restored, not just the one who had survived. And slowly, something shifted. I no longer introduced myself with hesitation. I no longer carried quiet shame into new spaces. I no longer braced for rejection in every connection. I began to live as Paulette, not as a memory of who I had been, but as a reflection of who Christ had made me. That's when I realized that healing had moved from something God had done in me to something God was now living through me.

Freedom is sustained through daily practices, not just occasional breakthroughs. Some of the most important practices are simple. Returning to truth when feelings rise. Choosing forgiveness again when old anger whispers. Letting the Father love you when independence tries to lead. Confessing fear instead of hiding it. Worshiping when your soul feels quiet. Sitting with God without trying to fix yourself.

Freedom grows where truth is practiced.

Even in freedom, feelings will still come and go. Some days you'll feel strong. Some days you'll feel tender. Some days you'll feel confident. Some days you'll feel unsure. But the truth remains steady: how I feel still does not reflect the truth. Your feelings are no longer your compass; the Holy Spirit is. You no longer walk forward as a survivor, an orphan, a prisoner, a mistake, or a question mark. You now walk forward as a new creation, a forgiven child, an adopted daughter or son, a cherished one, and a living testimony of grace. Your life now declares something powerful without needing to say a word: Jesus still restores.

Ask yourself honestly: Where are you tempted to live from your past instead of your identity? What boundaries do you need to strengthen? Which truth do you need to return to daily? Where is God inviting you to trust Him more deeply in freedom? Walking free isn't about perfection. It's about direction. Let's pray.

Jesus, You did not only heal me, you set me on a new path. Teach me how to walk as one who is free. Train my heart to return to truth quickly.

Strengthen my spirit when old patterns try to rise. Guard what You have restored. I do not walk alone. I do not walk backward. I do not walk in fear. I walk in freedom. In Your victorious name, Amen.

Here is the final truth of this journey:

You were created in God's image. Your identity was fractured by sin and pain. You were made new in Christ. You were freed through forgiveness. You were restored through adoption. Now, you walk free.

What I've written in these pages is not just something I believe, it is something I've had to live. What follows is part of that journey.

From Survival
to Surrender

I do not share my story often.

That is not because I am ashamed of what
Jesus has done in my life. It is because I
never want to give the enemy more
attention than he deserves; and he deserves
none. If I am going to tell any part of my
story, then my prayer is that people would
walk away seeing Christ and Christ alone.
Not my pain. Not my failures. Not what
was done to me. Not even what I have
walked through.

I want them to see Jesus.

I did not grow up in a Christian home. I
grew up with a general respect for the name
of God, but I did not grow up knowing
Him. My childhood was marked by things
no child should have to carry, alcohol,
instability, abandonment, fear, and abuse.
Some of my earliest years were shaped by
things I did not yet have language for, but
they left deep marks on my heart.

By the time I was old enough to understand that something was wrong, I had already begun to believe lies about myself.

I believed I was unwanted.
I believed I was unloved.
I believed I was alone.
I believed I existed to be hurt, overlooked, or used.

Those lies did not show up all at once. They were formed over years of brokenness, disappointment, trauma, and loss. Little by little, they settled deep into my heart until they started to feel like truth.

So, I learned how to survive.

I learned how to be strong. I learned how to protect myself. I learned how to carry things I was never meant to carry. I learned how to numb pain instead of face it. I learned how to keep moving, keep functioning, and keep people from seeing how broken I really was.

On the outside, I could keep going.
On the inside, I was falling apart.

Eventually, all that pain led me deeper into destructive choices. I drank heavily. I hated myself. I could not see value in my life. I felt like I did not belong anywhere. The more pain I carried, the more I tried to bury it, and the more I buried it, the more it grew.

What I thought would numb the pain only made it worse.

And then Jesus stepped in.

On October 10, 1990, I surrendered my heart to Jesus. I did not fully understand everything that was happening in that moment, but I knew He was drawing me. I knew something real had happened. I knew I had encountered the living Christ.

It was beautiful, and it was genuine.

But this is the part of my story that matters deeply to me now: meeting Jesus and being transformed by Him were not the same thing for me, at least not all at once.

I loved Him. I wanted Him. I was drawn to His presence. I got involved in church. I served. I went to Bible college. I learned doctrine. I did ministry. I was around the things of God.

But there were still places in me that remained untouched by surrender.

That was a painful realization.

I had believed that if I came to Jesus, everything would instantly be easy. I thought the struggle would disappear. I thought the pain would lose its voice overnight. I thought that if I was sincere enough, committed enough, involved enough, then I would stop feeling so broken.

But that was not my reality.

I still wrestled deeply with rejection, shame, fear, self-hatred, insecurity, and the old lies that had formed in me over the years.

For a long time, I did not understand why.

I loved Jesus, so why was I still struggling? I was in church, so why did I still feel stuck? I believed in God, so why did I still feel so broken?

What the Lord began to show me changed everything.

Proximity to Jesus is not the same as surrender.

I could be near Him without yielding fully to Him. I could sit in His presence and still hold tightly to control. I could sing, serve, attend, study, and do ministry while keeping certain places in my heart guarded from His touch.

I could love Him and still be terrified to let Him into the deepest wounds.

That was where the battle was.

There were parts of me that still believed I had to protect myself. There were parts of me that still felt safer staying in control. There were parts of me that did not know how to trust God with what had hurt me most.

I was near Jesus but not fully surrendered.

And then the Lord, in His mercy, began to confront the lies I had lived under for years.

He began to show me that the thoughts tormenting me were not His thoughts toward me. The words that echoed in my mind were not His voice. The accusations, the shame, the worthlessness, the rejection, the fear of abandonment, the belief that I was unlovable and unwanted, none of that came from Him.

That matters.

Because if the lie is in your mind, the only way to break it is with the truth.

Not positive thinking.
Not pretending.
Not trying harder.
Not changing your environment.
Not running somewhere else and hoping you can outrun your pain.

The only thing that breaks the power of a lie is the truth of God's Word.

So that is where the deep work began for me.

When I felt unwanted, I had to go to Scripture and remind myself that He chose me.

When I felt unloved, I had to return to the truth that I am loved by God.

When I felt like I did not belong, I had to anchor myself in the truth that I had been adopted into His family.

When I felt abandoned, I had to hold onto His promise that He would never leave me nor forsake me.

I wish I could say that I read those verses once and everything changed.

That is not how it happened.

I still felt the old feelings. I still heard the old lies. I still struggled. But I made the choice, repeatedly, to place the truth of God's Word above the voice of my emotions, above the voice of my history, and above the whispers of the enemy.

That is where transformation began.

Not when I suddenly felt better, but when I chose to believe what God said was true, even when my feelings had not yet caught up.

Somewhere in that process, I began to see
this same truth in Scripture, especially in
the lives of Peter and Judas.

Both men walked closely with Jesus.
Both were chosen.
Both heard His teaching.
Both saw the miracles.
Both lived in proximity to the Son of God.
And both failed.

Peter denied Jesus.
Judas betrayed Him.

Yet their stories did not end the same way.

Peter broke and turned back.
Judas felt remorse but did not return to
Jesus.

Peter brought his failure into the presence
of the One who could restore him.
Judas carried his failure away from the only
One who could heal him.

That distinction pierced me.

It forced me to ask myself:

Am I near Jesus… or surrendered to Him?

That question mattered then and it still matters now.

There came a point in my journey when I had to stop asking Jesus to fix everything around me and start surrendering everything within me.

Not polished.
Not put together.
Not pretending.

Just surrendered.

I do not share my story because I have arrived.
I do not share it because I have done everything right.
I do not share it because I have all the answers.

I share it because Jesus is faithful.

He is faithful to pursue us when we hide.
He is faithful to confront lies with truth.
He is faithful to meet us in our failure without rejecting us.
He is faithful to restore what we thought was beyond repair.

He is faithful to keep working in us when the process feels slow.
He is faithful not to leave us where He found us.

That is my story.

Yes, there was pain. Yes, there was brokenness. Yes, there were years of struggle, fear, bad decisions, partial surrender, and deep internal battles.

But that is not the truest thing about me.

The truest thing about me is this:

Jesus kept coming for me.

He kept calling.
He kept pursuing.
He kept speaking truth.
He kept extending mercy.
He kept inviting surrender.

And He still does.

If my story says anything, I pray it says this:

You can be near Jesus without being changed, but if you will surrender to Him fully, He will meet you there.

He does not ask you to clean yourself up first.
He does not ask you to have it all figured out.
He does not ask you to stop being broken before you come.

He simply asks you to come honestly, fully, and with open hands.

He can handle the places you are afraid to let Him touch.

He can speak truth louder than the lies you have believed.

He can restore what failure, sin, trauma, and shame have tried to define.

He can give you a new name where the world gave you wounds.

He can make you whole.

So, I share my story for one reason:

Not so you will see me, but so you will see Him.

He is the Redeemer.
He is the Restorer.
He is the One who still transforms.
And He is still doing that work in me.

An Invitation

If you have read this and you recognize yourself in any part of my story, the brokenness, the striving, the feeling of being near Jesus but not fully surrendered, then I want to speak to you for a moment. Jesus is not asking you to fix yourself before you come to Him. He is not asking you to have all the answers. He is not asking you to clean up your past. He is simply inviting you to surrender.

Not halfway.
Not when you feel ready.
Not when everything makes sense.
Now.

You may have known about Him for years. You may have even believed in Him. But the question is not, "Do I know about Jesus?"

The question is:
Have I given Him my life?
Have I stopped managing it on my own?
Have I stopped holding pieces back?
Have I surrendered?

If the answer is no, or even "I'm not sure", this is your moment. You don't need perfect words. You just need an honest heart.

A Prayer of Surrender

Jesus,

I come to You just as I am.

Not pretending.
Not hiding.
Not trying to fix myself first.

You see everything, the broken places, the pain, the fear, the things I've held onto for so long.

And today, I choose to surrender.

I believe that You are who You say You are.
I believe that You gave Your life for me.
And I believe that You are calling me to something more than the life I've been living.

So, I give You my life.

All of it.

The parts I understand, and the parts I don't.
The places that feel strong, and the places that feel completely broken.

Forgive me for trying to live on my own.
Forgive me for holding back.
Forgive me for believing lies instead of Your truth.

I choose You.

I choose to trust You. I choose to follow You.
I choose to surrender, fully.

Do in me what I cannot do on my own.

Heal what has been broken. Restore what has been lost. Replace every lie with Your truth.

From this moment forward, my life is Yours.

In Jesus' name,
Amen.

If You Took a Step Today

If you prayed this prayer, or if something in your heart shifted as you read these pages, I don't want you to walk this out alone.

Following Jesus was never meant to be done in isolation.

If you have questions, need prayer, or want help taking your next step, you are welcome to reach out. You can find me on Facebook at Redefined: Healing, Freedom, and Identity in Christ

While I may not be able to respond immediately to every message, I will do my best to read and pray over what is shared.

More importantly, I encourage you to get connected to a Bible-believing, Spirit-filled church where you can grow in truth, community, and relationship with Jesus.

A Final Word

You do not have to have everything figured out. You do not have to be perfect. You do not have to clean yourself up before you come to Him. Just come.

Jesus is not waiting for a better version of you.
He is inviting you, right now, as you are.

And if you will surrender your life to Him, fully and honestly, He will meet you there.

Scripture to Hold on To

"Though my father and mother forsake me, the Lord will receive me."
Psalm 27:10 (NIV)

"He who began a good work in you will carry it on to completion until the day of Christ Jesus."
Philippians 1:6 (NIV)

Epilogue
If You're Still in the Middle

If you are finishing this book and you still feel like you're "in the middle" of your healing, I want you to know this first and foremost: God is not in a rush with you. He is patient. He is kind. He is loving. He is not holding a stopwatch over your life. He is not disappointed that your healing is taking time. There is no secret deadline you are failing to meet.

Each of us is on a journey, and every journey is walked at its own pace. Even in the struggle—especially in the struggle—He has not abandoned you. If you still feel tired, stuck, or discouraged, hear this clearly: you are not a failure. You haven't done anything wrong. Needing time doesn't mean you're resisting God. It just means you're human.
Healing takes time. And that time is not wasted.

So be patient with yourself. If you need to rest, rest. If you need to pause, pause. And when you're ready, come back and take the next step. Don't give up. Your story is still unfolding. Your healing is still happening. Your transformation is still in motion.

And as you close this book, I want to leave you with one final truth to carry with you:

You are worth it.

If you'd like help continuing this journey, the Reader's Guide in the next section offers simple ways to reflect, pray, and walk these truths out in everyday life.

Reader's Guide
Walking it Out

This book is not meant to be rushed. It was written to be received.

Each chapter invites reflection, prayer, and honest engagement with the Holy Spirit. You may choose to move through one chapter each week, sit with certain sections longer, or return to chapters as the Spirit leads.

There is no "right" pace.
There is only your pace.

How to Use This Guide
After reading each chapter, take time, alone or with others, to reflect on the questions below. You may write your responses, pray through them quietly, or simply sit with God and listen.

Leave space.
Move Slowly.
Let truth settle.

Reflection Questions

What stood out to me most in this chapter?

What truth about God did I see more clearly?

What lie about me was confronted or exposed?

Where do I sense the Holy Spirit inviting me to respond?

What is one small step of obedience I can take this week?

You may walk this journey alone, with a trusted friend, or within a small group. However you walk it, remember:

This is not about perfection.
It is about **becoming.**

Continuing the Journey

If you would like to go deeper, *Redefined* also has a companion study designed for personal reflection or group discussion. It offers guided questions, Scripture exploration, and practical next steps to help you continue walking in your identity, healing, and freedom in Christ.

Declarations
For Identity, Freedom, And Belonging

These declarations are not meant to be recited mechanically. They are meant to train the heart.

You may speak these aloud, pray them quietly, or journal through them slowly. Return to them as often as needed. Let truth take root.

Identity Declarations

> I am created in the image of God.
> I am not an accident.
> I am not my trauma.
> I am not my past.

I am who God says I am.
I am chosen, seen, and known.
I am not disqualified.
I am becoming who God designed me
to be.

New Creation Declarations

I am a new creation in Christ.
My old life no longer defines me.
The cross has the final word over my
identity.
My past has lost its authority.
Resurrection life lives in me.
Dead things no longer lead my life.
Christ is my source.

Forgiveness Declarations

I release what I no longer need to
carry.
I place justice in God's hands.
Bitterness does not protect me.
Forgiveness frees me.
I am no longer defined by offense.
My heart is learning how to let go.
Freedom belongs to me in Christ.

Adoption & Belonging Declarations

I am adopted into God's family.

I am not an orphan.

I am wanted by God.

I belong to Him.

I am not on probation.

I am not easily replaced.

I am cherished.

I am safe to rest.

A Daily Prayer for Walking Free

Jesus,
Today I choose truth over feelings.
I choose trust over fear.
I choose forgiveness over control.
I choose identity over shame.

Teach me to walk as one who is free.
Guard what You have restored.
Silence every lie that tries to rise again.

I belong to You.
I am becoming.
I walk in freedom today.

Amen.

About the Author

Paulette Toews serves as an Assistant Pastor in Connecticut, where she walks with others through preaching, teaching, discipleship, and pastoral care. Her heart is to help people discover their identity in Christ and walk in the freedom He gives.

Redefined was written out of that same desire, to point people to Jesu and the truth of who they are in Him.

Made in United States
North Haven, CT
24 May 2026

11323397R00050